A Chanticleer Press Edition
Pictures collected and edited by
Milton Rugoff and Ann Guilfoyle
Commentary by Ann and Myron Sutton
Photographs by Tom Algire, Ron Austing,
William A. Bake, Jr., Les Blacklock, Jim Bones,
Dennis Brokaw, Richard Weymouth Brooks,
Dean Brown, Fred Bruemmer, Ed Bry,
Sonja Bullaty & Angelo Lomeo,
James H. Carmichael, Jr., Patricia Caulfield,
David Cavagnaro, Ron Church, Ed Cooper,
Steve Crouch, William G. Damroth,
Thase Daniel, Jack Dermid, Douglas Faulkner,

A Photographic Celebration of Unspoiled

the WILD

Andreas Feininger, Jerry Gentry,
Ray O. Green, Philip Hyde, Les Line, Yvona &
Momo Momatiuk, David Muench, Charlie Ott,
Robert Perron, Willis Peterson, Eliot Porter,
Betty Randall, Bill Ratcliffe, Leonard Lee Rue III,
Caulion Singletary, Gordon Smith,
Charles Steinhacker, Kojo Tanaka,
James P. Valentine, Bradford Washburn,
Ralph Weiss, Larry West, Steven C. Wilson,
Don Worth, Michael Wotton

Harper & Row, Publishers
New York · Evanston · San Francisco · London

America
PLACES

1. First frontispiece: Aerial view of sunset on a tidal flat in the Mississippi delta (Robert Perron)

2. Second frontispiece: Detail of prairie grass (Patricia Caulfield)

3. Third frontispiece: Musk oxen (Kojo Tanaka)

The Wild Places:
A Photographic Celebration of Unspoiled America

First Edition   Second Printing 1974
Library of Congress Catalog Card Number: 73-1075
SBN: 06-014176-X

The photographs of the winter wren and the parula warbler by Eliot Porter are from the book *Birds of North America* by Eliot Porter, published in 1972 by E. P. Dutton & Co., Inc., and are used with their permission

Prepared and produced by Chanticleer Press, Inc.
Staff of this book:
Publisher: Paul Steiner
Editor: Milton Rugoff
Picture editor: Ann Guilfoyle
Production: Gudrun Buettner, Helga Lose
Design: Massimo Vignelli

Printed and bound by Amilcare Pizzi, S.p.A., Milan, Italy

Contents

Foreword

There is a standing joke among dwellers in the Blue Ridge Mountains that when fog and clouds roll over the ridges, sift dramatically through the forest, and swirl in great arcs over the high country, the most common question asked by travelers is: "How do we get down off this mountain?"

When thunder crashes over the darkened ridges and torrents of rain sweep through thickets of buckeye, among the human beings likely to remain on the summits—or at least to emerge from the shelter of an overhang—are the wildland photographers.

Because of this persistence of vision, as it were, the photographer is capable of bringing us an America most people never see. Indeed, visitors abandon the high peaks at some of nature's finest moments, but the photographer often not only rushes there if he happens to be nearby when storms strike, but he has the equipment to capture the scene and bring it back. There is a certain element of luck, to be sure, as when the clouds open to admit a shaft of sunlight in just the right location, or when a pair of white-tail bucks leap across a meadow in front of the camera. But for the most part the professional photographer of wild scenes must make a picture rather than "take" it. He looks for the revelatory angle that others than artists might miss. He has the time and patience to wait for the right composition of light and shadow. His telescopic lenses bring into focus what the human eye alone cannot perceive. And his knowledge of weather and plant and animal life takes him to significant places at times when nature is most active or most magnificent. Against the challenge of insects, fog, cold rain, rough weather, snow, high winds and blowing dust, the photographer sets up his equipment and composes sensitive interpretations of the natural world.

And that is what this book is about, the real America, specifically the wilder parts of the continent. While most of its wilderness has been lost, the United States is by no means so badly damaged that its citizens cannot take great pleasure from the remaining—and still vast—wild spaces. These tell us something of what the original pristine land was like, and even though most people seldom see such wilderness areas, they are as much a part of our vision of America as anything that man has made. Through the photographer's lenses we are introduced to them intimately, poetically, and in unexpected ways.

This book is also about some of the earliest inhabitants on the continent—the wild animals. Only a small fraction of them is pictured, but the representatives are diverse and striking, from those that live by hunting and fishing, as do the bears of Alaska and birds of Florida, to those that graze or browse, such as deer.

It is not necessarily a "good" world that is depicted here, nor altogether a "beautiful" one, since good and bad have little or no ecological significance in the context of the wild outdoors. Rather, this book celebrates natural America as it still exists, and contributes to the continuing need to remind ourselves and our children of the immense inheritance we possess.

The pictures represent the best work of forty-seven of the leading photographers of the natural world. In making their selection, the editors screened over 40,000 pictures with immense care and discrimination—in itself a herculean feat. What is particularly impressive is how fresh many of the pictures seem, how far from the standard views that most tourists have seen or that postcards have made familiar.

The thirty-one natural niches presented here are only a sampling of the hundreds that might have been included. Who can say how many more volumes would be needed to do justice to a land as varied as the United States? But apologies are hardly necessary for as magnificent a collection of pictures as this.

The arrangement of picture units follows to a large degree the natural arrangement of surface features of the land. As is perhaps fitting, the photographs of Alaska, that grand and fragile land whose places are wilder than all the rest, come at the head of the book. The sequence then proceeds in a broad swath down the western United States, moving along the coast and through the Sierra Nevada and the canyonlands to the deserts, up through the continental heartland to the north woods, eastward to Maine and down the eastern states and the Atlantic Coast through rich southern swamps to a spectacular finale—the fragile, precious Everglades at the tip of southern Florida.

In our commentary on each of these photographic glimpses we have tried to offer some thoughts on those first and profound fundamentals in an appreciation of nature's majesty: the geologic wonders of rock and erosion, and the almost miraculous ecological relationships between wild plants and animals and their environment.

Here then is a microcosm on paper that encompasses as well as a book can do it the vast macrocosm of wildness that lies beyond ourselves. It is a study of the great and the small, the complex and the simple, the past, the present, the future. May these words and pictures serve as an introduction to the real America. And may the mountains, forest, shores and life depicted here remain as places of escape and renewal to be prized forever.

Ann Sutton

Myron Sutton

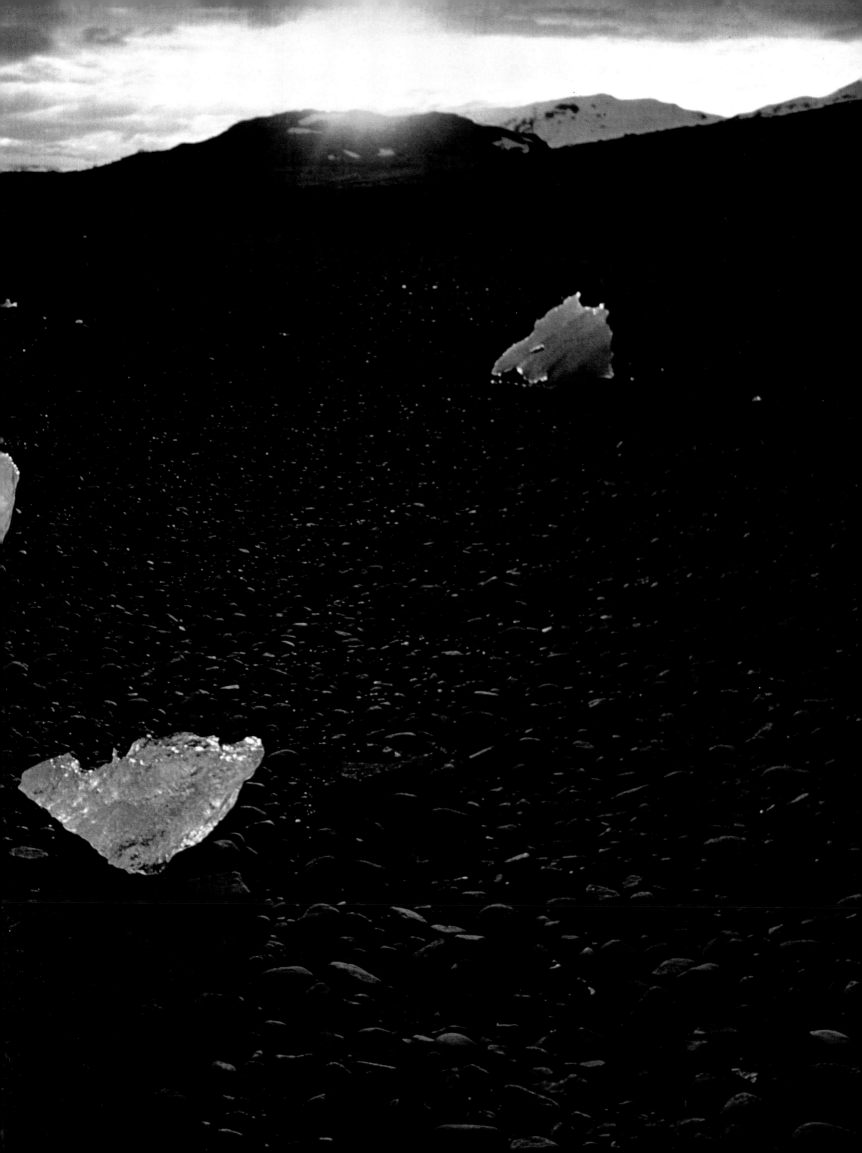

Images of Alaska

*Photographed by Dean Brown, Fred Bruemmer,
Ed Cooper, Philip Hyde, Charlie Ott, Kojo
Tanaka, Bradford Washburn, and Michael Wotton*

For all of Alaska's immensity, many who go there
have a sense of coming home. It is a curious feeling,
as though we heard the "call of the wild," or
were webbed in some kind of evolutionary magic
millenniums before we were born. Neither the
bigness of its mountains, nor the cruelty of its cold,
nor the enormous distances awe us oppressively.
We are drawn to this land not for what we want it
to be, or out of a desire to change it, but on its own
terms as enduring wilderness.

Untamed, unbridled, nearly undisturbed, Alaska
combines the noblest characteristics of California,
New Zealand, and the Patagonian Andes, but is so
much larger that it seems almost endless. And
something always seems to be happening: volcanic
eruptions, landslides, avalanches, earthquakes,
tidal waves, or sprawling storms whose lightning
bolts leave thousands of acres of forest and tundra
afire. Glaciers crack and boom and calve at the
water's edge, dispatching waves of sound and waves
of water that reverberate between the shores of
rock-bound inlets. Trickles from melting mountain
ice packs gather in torrents and tumble downstream
as gray-brown seething waters filled with glacially
scoured fine rock powder.

We step onto a mat of sphagnum moss and sink to
our knees in its cushioned softness—but up
comes a layer of mosquitoes that nearly blots out the
horizon. Or, in a summer riot of color, Alaska
blazes with the magenta of fireweed, and the tundra
produces forget-me-nots, saxifrages, monkshoods,
bluebells, daisies, arnicas, phlox and cottongrass.
Long days end in prolonged sunsets, and a purple
alpenglow remains on snow peaks for hours.
Whales leap out of the water. Gulls sing disjointed
choruses. Puffins flash through the air. Grizzlies
paw for roots or slap fish out of streams.

And then, above the tundra, the world becomes
much less hospitable to life. The gravel, the naked
ridges, the caribou bull silhouetted on a forward
point, the beginning of snow, the white sweeps
upward, and finally Mt. McKinley, highest point in
North America. There images lead the mind up to
the stars. But the stars do not breathe with life,
unless they too have ridges where sheep may roam,
and clear sharp air in which eagles may fly.

8

10

11

12

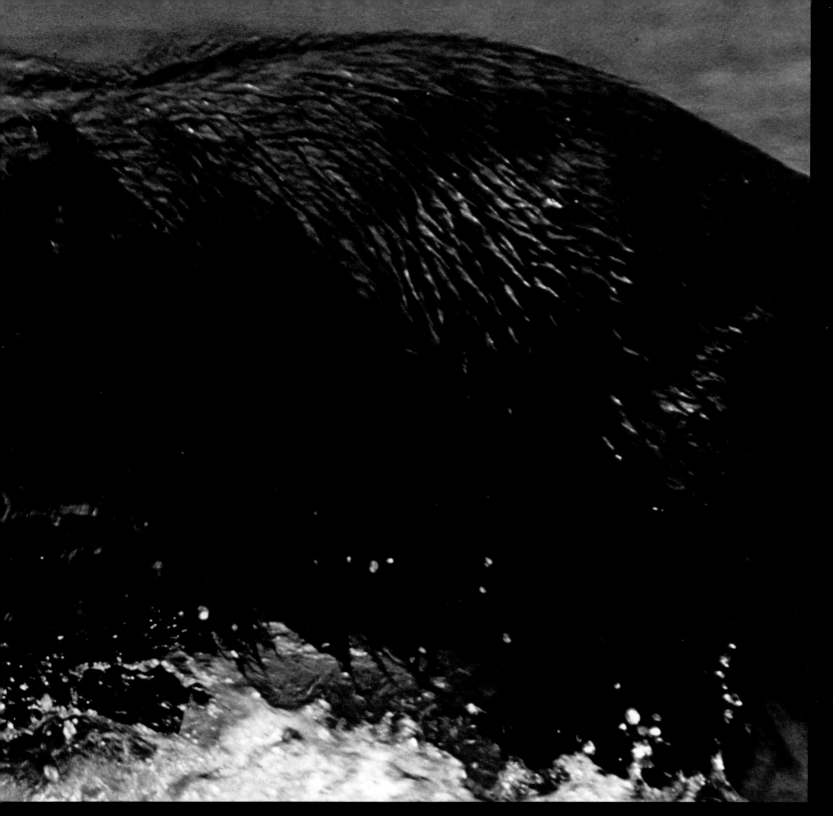

19

Rain Forest

Photographed by Dennis Brokaw and Betty Randall

21. Rain forest in the Hoh River area of Olympic National Park, Washington (Dennis Brokaw)

22. Trees covered with mosses, lichens and ferns in rain forest, Olympic National Park (Betty Randall)

Of all the miles of rich moist coastal forest along the edge of the continent between Alaska and California, few can match those of the Hoh River, which drains out of Washington's Olympic Mountains. Sitka spruce, so dominant from Alaska south, reaches its maximum size here in a specimen more than fifty feet in circumference. Along the rain forest trails in Olympic National Park, one can walk beneath Sitka spruce 300 feet tall, great towers of life that were born three centuries before Columbus.

Little wonder that the trees reach epic proportions. In this peaceful land they are assailed by little more than drifting mist, with the rain at times only a filtered drizzle that scarcely dampens one's jacket. Yet downpours do occur, and 150 inches of moisture fall into this forest each year, sustaining not only tall trees but numerous varieties of other plants, including approximately seventy species of mosses and seventy species of lichens.

No green anywhere surpasses the vivid hues in this forest. Leaves of vine and bigleaf maples, the latter as much as a foot across, catch soft white light coming through spruce and fir and transform it into a rich yellow-green. Limbs curve over like arches in churches and are festooned with cushions and waving curtains of moss. Thick layers of vegetation cover the forest floor and downed trees, and become seed beds for other life. In fact, plants growing profusely on the limbs of trees may eventually reach such large size and catch so much water that they break off the limbs that support them.

In such an earthly paradise, animals thrive, from slugs in the moss to wrens among upturned roots, to Olympic elk on the meadows. Man can do little more than stand back and admire the complex mechanisms at work in this temperate rain forest, one of the most harmoniously balanced natural environments in North America.

Spawning Time

Photographed by Steven C. Wilson

Each year that immensely mysterious process, salmon spawning, takes places in the waters of the Northwest. Anadromous fish, those that return to fresh water to lay their eggs, travel at great hardship and risk to reach their spawning grounds—which may be in coastal estuaries or hundreds of miles upstream. Certain salmon, for example, travel relentlessly for more than two months, day and night, without stopping to rest, without eating, without any other thought than to reach those shallow riffles where they were born and to which they must commit their eggs and sperm.

Those that arrive at all—after fighting the current upstream for more than 800 miles and climbing to an elevation of some 6,000 feet above the level of the sea—arrive utterly exhausted. The females sweep aside gravel in broad stream-bottom nests and deposit thousands of eggs, which are fertilized by the males. After the process is complete, the journey ends in the death of the worn-out, depleted adults.

Come winter, the eggs hatch out, and after a year of growth, tens of thousands of young may swim downstream toward the sea. How this seemingly miraculous process functions is still mainly a mystery to men. Unfortunately, the number of fish engaged in such journeys has vastly decreased where men have dammed or polluted the streams. But cleaning and conservation of river habitats may save from destruction these delicate spawning systems, thus preserving one of the most remarkable of biological phenomena.

23

25

26

Redwood Kingdom

Photographed by David Muench and Don Worth

These fragile vales look delicate, defenseless, destructible. Yet nothing that nature does to them, neither fire nor lightning nor disease, seems able to alter the redwood community. Trees of this genus have been here for at least 140 million years, and if man controls those fatal instruments, the saw and the bulldozer, they may remain for another 140 million years.

Each tree grows for centuries in this gentle, humid environment not far from the Pacific Coast. Mist shrouds the tree tops much of the time, and the mild offshore masses of air produce a relatively stable climate without extremes. New trees sprout largely from burls, and may live for more than 2,000 years, reaching record heights. One redwood, at 367 feet, is the tallest known living thing. Surprisingly, the roots go down no more than six feet; however, they radiate more than a hundred feet from the base of the trunk.

Thanks to the abundant moisture, a luxuriant ecosystem occurs beneath the trees. Ferns unveil their fronds from deep humus. Pink-flowered oxalis proliferates in patches on the forest floor. Red alder, azalea and rhodondendron constitute the next higher level of foliage. Animals exist—deer, moles, salamander, birds and others—but usually only in limited numbers; there is simply too much shade to produce the kinds of food most creatures prefer.

The region of coast redwoods is not very widespread. Some of the best groves are preserved as national parks and monuments and California state parks, and in them man may contemplate the antiquity of a world in which he is but a newcomer. His temples and cathedrals somewhat resemble these redwood groves, but when we observe a great forest of them, we know that man makes nothing like them. He is only beginning to understand the laws that govern both them and him.

Pacific Shores

Photographed by Steven C. Wilson and Don Worth

31. Cape Johnson in Olympic National Park on the Washington coast (Steven C. Wilson)

32. Eroded rock on the shore near Pescadero, California (Don Worth)

33. Coastal area of Olympic National Park (Steven C. Wilson)

When roiling storms from the Pacific Ocean swirl landward, they strike the coast undiminished. If their fury is not as intense as that of eastern hurricanes, they do stir up enormous waves and send them crashing into cliffs with sufficient energy to modify the coast. A wave once hurled against Trinidad Head, California, reached a height of more than 200 feet. Abundant energy is also present in the coastal currents, which transport sand and drifting logs, and tumble them up on wild and lonely beaches.

Salt spray, fog, cold wind—it would seem almost a test of endurance for life to survive in such an environment. Moreover, the Pacific border is our most unstable seacoast. As judged by present-day measurements and by old beaches now high and dry, the land is slowly but steadily rising out of the sea. Earth movements break off rocks, whole cliffs, or sections of land that tumble into the surf and are battered to pieces by the waves. If prolonged rains soak the slippery soil on hills above the coast, great masses of mud and rock can come loose and slide off into the waters.

If the land stops temporarily, on its way to the sea, it becomes a settlement ground for seeds, and growth proceeds despite the perils of salt, storm and instability. Fields of white and yellow lupine spread across the wind-chilled slopes, as do succulents, sand verbena and wax myrtle. On the forwardmost craggy cliffs are Monterey cypresses that cling in what may seem like a duel with the elements. But the trees hang on in highly precipitous locations, and even act somewhat as a buffer for prolific though less hardy Monterey pines inland. Together with battered but thriving grasses and herbaceous plants that grow along the coast, and animal life on rocks and in tide pools at the surf, these species illustrate the awesome tenacity of life in the face of extremes.

Tidal Pools and Tidal Waters

Photographed by Dennis Brokaw and Ron Church

34. Tide pool (upper middle zone) containing chiefly algae and periwinkles, Point Lobos, California

35. Limpets and closed anemones in a tidal area at Pebbly Beach, Point Lobos

36. Eroded sandstone and tide-washed pebbles at Pebbly Beach

37. Tide pool (middle to lower zone) showing anemones, sea urchins, chitons, algae, encrusting sponge, and tiny red "spiders" (34–37 by Dennis Brokaw)

38. Moray eel

39. Pacific white perch in kelp bed

40. California sea lions

41. Smooth brown turban kelp snail

42. Garibaldi (38–42 by Ron Church)

If we could ask some of the animals that cling to rocks at the ocean's edge whether the Pacific was pacific, they would need only the next impact of tons of salt-laden sea to answer in their behalf. Indeed, we can surmise from their heavy shells, tough and resistant skins, gripping tube feet, and strong attachment devices what it takes to stay in place and keep alive under the incessant battering of powerful waves.

Mussels, barnacles and sea stars live high enough on the shore to bear the full force of the waves. Farther down are predacious worms and worms that assemble in colonies. There is also more delicate and fragile life, but it is resilient and seems not to suffer from being tossed around. Sea anemones, for example, open their brightly colored tentacles to screen out the waters for fresh arrivals of food. Descending some more, we find sea urchins, crabs, cucumbers, limpets, chitons, sponges and snails. Great curtains of kelp, a little farther from shore, smooth out the waters to some degree. They harbor sea otters at the surface and such residents as the gold garibaldi, an abundant fish, and red abalone, a mollusk, below.

Sea lions, best known for their barking on offshore rocky islets, seem to have little trouble with the crashing sea. When swept away they roll with the waves and swim down along the face of the rocky coast.

In such a relentlessly pounded domain, no life is permanent, nor even the land itself. The swirling waves pluck pebbles from the sand, or rocks from the cliffs, and fling them endlessly against the shore, slowly wearing the land away. Every cycle of tides whirls pebbles in potholes around and around, grinding down pits in the rock. All this dramatically supports the geologist's conviction that one of the greatest forces on earth is moving water.

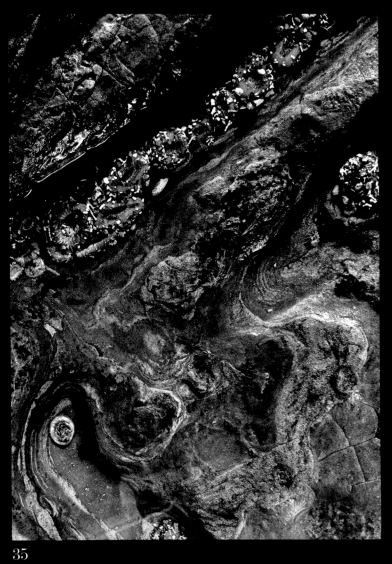

35

41

It looks as though nature had ripped these peaks from their moorings, thrust them above 13,000 feet, and then stopped. The mountains are so solid, the change so hard to detect, that men might call them eternal. But the Sierra Nevada is not eternal, and nature has not stopped anything. Occasional tremblings at the surface, accompanied by grinding, crashing landslides, reveal how the rocks below are still adjusting to stresses within the earth. High winds, deep snows, and avalanches all have their effect on the forest and rock.

Yet every spring the poppies roll up the canyon slopes in incandescent carpets. Redbuds burst into magenta bloom. Dogwoods spread their creamy white flowers on the valley floors while shooting stars spring up in purple masses on highland flats. Melting snow sends singing, roaring torrents down the rock-strewn gorges and in spring the canyons echo with a roar of water plunging hundreds of feet, dissolving into spray, swirling around the wet gray rocks, and finally splashing on the slopes below. There is little moisture after that. The forest dries out to tinder in summer. The streams diminish and the falls dry up. Yet lilies persist in sheltered vales and azaleas bloom even while their leaves are turning cinnamon brown.

At summer's end the color of oaks and aspens spills down the slopes like a flow of molten gold. The air is peaceful and quiet, except that soon a September storm roars across the domes and spires in angry waves of roiling black clouds, and lightning

44

45

46

Wild in the Rockies

Photographed by Kojo Tanaka

The upsweep of rock, edging thousands of square miles of prairie, is all the more dramatic for its sudden rise from flatness to elevations of more than 14,000 feet. Few foothills provide transition. Suddenly there are "flatirons," great slabs of rock pushed up on end, and above them soaring granites and schists, part of a continental chain—the Cordilleran System—that extends from Alaska to Argentina. The peaks have familiar names, such as Longs and Pikes peaks, and the Wind River, Gros Ventre and Bitterroot mountains. But the native wildlife is not so often seen by man, principally because he seldom climbs the towering crags on which they dwell, or visits remote ravines in which they find the solitude they need.

The life of mountain goats, as an example, is easy enough, despite the cold and the snow, and when they get enough grass or foliage they lie at ease on a ledge, soaking up what warmth the sun provides. More often seen by man are Rocky Mountain mule deer, especially on meadows at dawn, near the edge of the forest. A shriek and a bright blue flash of wings in the woods herald an arriving Steller's jay, and a gray-black-white streak overhead is the Clark's nutcracker sailing from the limbs of some tall spruce or fir out over the mountain ridges and patches of ice.

Beneath the lodgepole pines, black bears move among the blueberries, consuming their fill. Wild strawberries, dogwoods, lupines, harebells, and honeysuckle provide not only colorful flowers but food for other members of the ecosystem, such as grouse, insects, hummingbirds and chipmunks. The high, wild tundra, fragile and at the margin of survival for certain organisms, is nevertheless an intricate life system mostly well adapted to environmental extremes of summit peaks.

Much remains unknown about the relation of cordilleran animals to their habitat. As the great Rocky Mountain naturalist Enos Mills once said: "I often wish that an old beaver neighbor of mine would write the story of his life."

Yellowstone

Photographed by Charles Steinhacker

Hot springs steam and ponds still boil as they always have. Each day the geysers continue to disgorge thousands of gallons of superhot water. And the Firehole River is nearly as pure and clear as it was when the first park rangers rode out on the trail to Thorofare Country a century ago. The miracle is that every species of wild animal existing then still lives along the upper Yellowstone River. Pelicans and trumpeter swans nest on secluded lakes. More than 250 grizzly bears, 500 bison, 15,000 elk, and goodly numbers of black bear, pronghorns, bighorns, coyotes and moose inhabit the mountains and meadows. Those rarest of rare, the wolf and mountain lion, so efficiently persecuted in the days when ecological principles were less well known, not only still hang on but may be slowly increasing. Thus more than any of America's wilder places, Yellowstone, the world's first national park, is a testimonial to the persistence of some men in conserving a portion of the original planet they inherited.

To see it best, one ought to go there in April or May while the snow is deep. At that season the grizzlies are emerging and running down elk, feeding on carcasses, or digging up roots in the valleys where snow has begun to melt. Elk roam along the Yellowstone River and can be seen by the thousands against dramatic backdrops of snow-covered cliffs and ice-filled ravines. On lonesome white flats long lines of hoofprints show the wanderings of bighorns as they search for sunny green slopes and the new grass of spring.

When summer does approach, the flowers bloom higher and higher, like an ascending wave of color, until in August they meet the melting snows of upper elevations. So brief is the season there that the plants fairly burst into bloom—harebells, yampa, lupine, phlox, monkshood, and a host of others.

Free of man's domination, Yellowstone has many wonders. Tiny life forms in alpine rivulets—or in boiling springs. Golden meadows of dwarf willows. A soft wind scented by spruce and pine. The crystalline glitter of volcanic glass. Or the echoing voices of cranes in flight across mountain marshes. Here men may glimpse the world as it was before they came and as it will be when they are gone.

The Rocks of Time

Photographed by Richard Weymouth Brooks and Ed Cooper

If the labyrinth through which Theseus pursued the Minotaur was as complicated as some of those in the canyonlands of Utah he might never have returned to Ariadne. For one thing, he would have needed a great deal more than a simple string to guide him— he would have needed wings to go up cliffs and escape box canyons or to descend from promontories and take up the trail again. Depending on how superstitious he was, he might have been delayed by rock shapes like totems and stone gods, phalanxes of goblins and gargoyles, by strange writings, friezes and other deductions of the human imagination. He could have wandered for days, confronted by the turbulent, winding Colorado River, pursuing old animal trails, hiding out in cottonwood thickets—all in all a red rock hegira perhaps even beyond the experience of the gods of Greece.

In the Canyonlands nearly everything is on a wide-open monumental scale. The "standing rocks" cover a space of thousands of square miles and a time span of millions of years of water erosion in an arid land. There are circular "upheaval domes," valleys underlain by salt, natural stone arches, stream-worn bridges, "fin" canyons separated by walls so thin that it looks as though the next wind might bring them down, and prairies that terminate in spectacular views of strange stone "cities" below. It is a geologic paradise, as though some textbook had been laid open to explain nearly every process of erosion and deposition, past and present. Today the inhabitants are chiefly coyotes, chipmunks and antelope ground squirrels, but there is abundant evidence in the form of cliff dwellings, granaries and pictographs that early men occupied much of the area, mazes and all.

If Theseus, too, had visited here, he might have returned to Crete with the news that here was a place fit for the gods.

The Depths of Time: Grand Canyon Country

Photographed by David Muench

61. Colorado River below Toroweap View, Grand Canyon National Monument, Arizona

62. Sunset over the Grand Canyon as seen from Bright Angel point looking toward South Rim and San Francisco Peaks

63. Westward view from Hopi Point, Grand Canyon

In few places is water so scarce yet so master of everything as on the Colorado Plateau. Water shapes and polishes, sculptures, transports, destroys and nourishes. Not only does it freeze in cracks, expand as ice, and thereby dislodge bits of cliffs, but relentlessly it pursues the fallen fragments, undermining them in floods, then splitting them again and again by freezing and thawing, dissolving them, and finally carrying the sediments to the sea. On the way, it leaps over travertine cliffs and falls into pools of aquamarine, descends from one wide terrace to another, laves the roots of cottonwood and willow, and bathes the wild green celery and purple orchids that grow along stream banks. Coots float on it. Muskrats live in it. Even bighorns leave their dry and rocky crags in search of seeps.

The music of falling water is amplified by the curving walls of coves into which it drips. In shadowed places it mirrors the sky, absorbing either the brilliant yellow of sunrise, or the blue of midday, or a lone sunbeam that manages to get through a cleft high above.

All temporary. Tomorrow's colors and tomorrow's cliffs and tomorrow's crystal pools will be a little different from what they were today—or yesterday.

Death Valley

Photographed by David Muench

Once there were lakes in scores of Southwestern basins. And Death Valley is no exception. The evidence is in the wave-cut cliffs on valley slopes, in the accumulations of saline sediments that remain as sharp-edged flats of salt, or the brackish pools with pupfish in them, remnants of a widespread fish fauna.

Today the land is dry and often searingly hot. Mud flats crack, dry up and blow away. Dunes form and reform, obedient to the desert breeze. Scant rains, scarcely an inch or two a year, may fall in torrents that roll all sizes of rocks toward the valley floor. Hardy plants like holly, cactus and creosote bush hang on to life even though no rain falls for months or perhaps even years, and manage to endure high heat approaching 200° near the surface.

At dusk the heat diminishes, and by dawn the temperature becomes more moderate. The desert at that hour is much less hostile to man, or not even hostile at all, its colors richer and the profiles of its dunes and mountains more pronounced. For the observant visitor there is never a dull moment between extremes of high temperature and low. Floods occur. Snow falls. High winds shake the creosote bush and hurl aloft great clouds of fine dust. At such times the bighorn sheep, coyotes, kit foxes, bobcats, lizards and other wildlife either bear the brunt of nature on the rampage or seek what cover they can.

Happily, the size of Death Valley National Monument, nearly 3,000 square miles, provides for the animals an ample protected domain in which to roam. It also attests to the compassion of man in saving an immense domain once unwanted and known as a deadly barrier to human exploration

64

66

Fields of Light

Photographed by David Cavagnaro

As the sun fills nature's meadows with light, and the plants convert this incoming radiant energy to tons of food, each meadow becomes a milieu of animal life. In thick grass stands, where gentians and geraniums grow so closely together they cover the ground, mice and rats make runways through the tangle. Sometimes the vegetation is so dense that we cannot see the runways, but coyotes and foxes can, and marsh hawks soar on silent wings in search of a ground squirrel foolishly exposed. Even smaller types of life thrive in the meadow. Insects inhabit the air, the plants and the soil, and spiders spin webs of geometric complexity and symmetry. Perhaps it is the simple beauty of the meadow that most impresses men. Light passing through translucent seeds can be akin to the light through a stained-glass window. A milkweed pod releasing its seeds to the wind tells a great deal more about biological history than men have yet been able to understand. In beads of moisture strung like pearls on a spider's web, in water drops with the world reflected in their spherical prisms, or in winter crystals of frost that divide the white of the early sun into golds, greens, reds and blues, there is infinite natural art.

And meadow music? The phoebe delivers a plaintive call. A bluebird's song, like that of the solitaire, remains discreet and delicate. The bobolink's bubbling notes are uttered from outpost stalks. But the meadowlark, whose resonant, poetic tones seem not of one voice but many, and the sandhill crane, whose quivering whistles echo across high mountain fields, are among the most memorable musical trademarks of wild America.

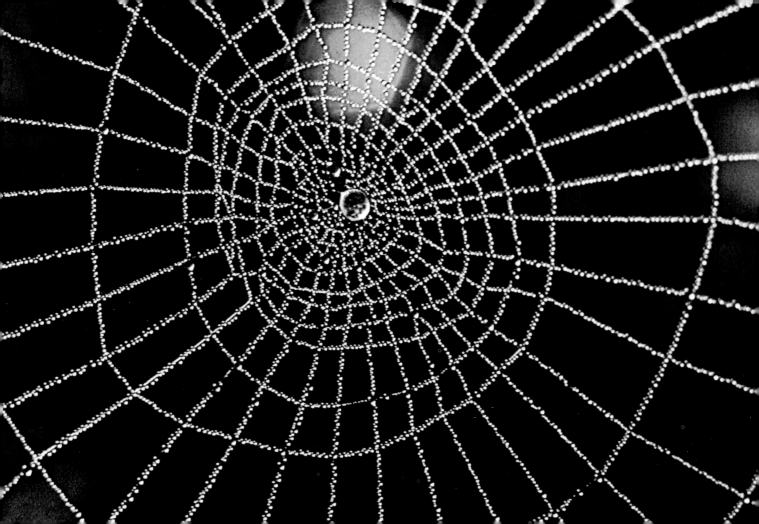

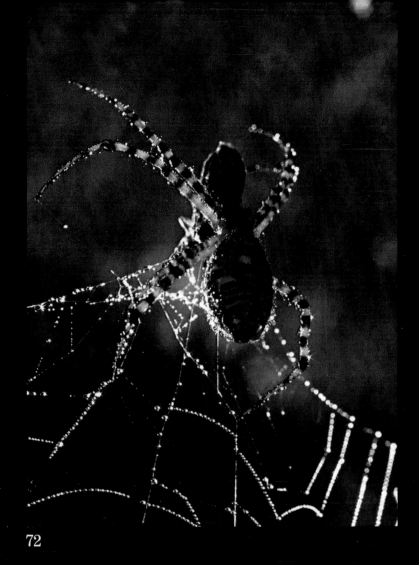

72

The Desert's Many Faces

Photographed by Steve Crouch and David Muench

75. *Sand dunes near Yuma, Arizona (Steve Crouch)*

76. *Spring flowers with the volcanic crest of the Ajo Mountains in the distance, Organ Pipe Cactus National Monument, Arizona*

77. *Spring poppies and creosote bush in Antelope Valley, Mojave Desert, southern California*

78. *The clay slopes of Blue Mesa, Petrified Forest National Park, Arizona (76-78 by David Muench)*

Given the right conditions of moisture, thousands of square miles of arid land from Texas to California burst into bloom each spring, defying the dry desert air and burning sun. Countless poppies, daisies, yuccas, cactuses and other species open up delicate flowers, as though there had never been any drought or dust. Even on shifting sands, sunflowers quickly sprout and grow and produce their seeds before the next high winds can cover them up.

Some dry deserts have few gardens—the badland types where soils are not conducive to growth—but these are atypical, and rare is the patch of desert that hasn't at least a sprig of grass.

This seeming anomaly of aridity and dense vegetation is answered by adaptations, the evolutionary adjustments that have fitted each organism for life under special conditions. In certain cases, of course, no water, no flower: the plant simply fails to germinate. In others, the blossoms appear even during protracted droughts. The seeds of some species are rolled and scratched and torn open by floods, an aid to sprouting at an obviously propitious time—and the coincidence is not accidental; while the floodwaters evaporate and the muddy terrain dries out, the plants get a very good start in life.

Still other species have been modified over the millenniums to hold on to precious moisture and not let it evaporate. The whiplike ocotillo simply loses its leaves; but when rains fall, even in unusual times like autumn, the ocotillo is fully covered with bright green leaves within three or four days.

The cactuses seem even better prepared. They store up water in their succulent trunks (a good-sized saguaro can weigh more than ten tons), and even when considerably shriveled for lack of rain, they still produce flowers.

But for all their adaptations, the plants of arid regions are vulnerable. Snow falls on the desert occasionally, and cold snaps lasting for several days

75

Life in a Dry Country

Photographed by Jerry Gentry, Thase Daniel, Willis Peterson, and Steven C. Wilson

Exuberance. The Gila woodpecker flies up to a hole in a giant saguaro cactus and feeds its young. The elf owl swoops down at dusk in search of insects. A tarantula scurries from its rocky hideout and attacks a beetle. Frogs produce filaments of eggs in puddles that are likely to evaporate before very long.

Perhaps the exuberance of desert life is due to the necessity of taking sudden and complete advantage of rain when it falls. Some organisms, in fact, complete an entire life cycle of eggs to adults to eggs again before the puddles dry up.

Part of the exuberance is due to a limited number of daylight hours when it is comfortable to be outside; hence the life processes must be confined to fewer hours of the day. Since the surface approaches 200° in the hottest part of the afternoon, most animals keep to their burrows or go to sleep in a shady place, reserving morning and evening hours for their peregrinations. A "night shift" comes on after the sun goes down—nighthawks, kit foxes, mice, rats, reptiles and other species adapted to cooler temperatures and absence of sunlight.

Thus there is hardly a moment when something is not astir, and one of the best representatives of the desert's vigor is the house finch. Its rapid, intricate songs, no matter how dry the weather, are delivered with a gusto and verve that seem to drain all the energy from its body. With that kind of exuberance, it is little wonder that the desert biome is one of nature's most active, well-developed communities.

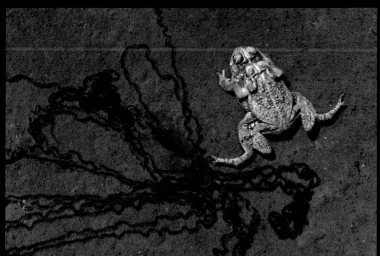

Texas: The Wide Land

Photographed by Jim Bones

85. *View near the mouth of Santa Elena Canyon on the Rio Grande, Big Bend National Park, Texas*

86. *Foggy dawn over the Edwards Plateau of central Texas, with prickly-pear cactus in the foreground and live oaks and cedar elms in the background*

87. *Texas bluebonnets, the Texas state flower, on the Edwards Plateau*

88. *Walking stick insect on bark*

89. *The central Texas hills in the Devil's Backbone country in autumn*

90. *View up Barton Creek Valley in the Edwards Plateau*

Texas is a crossroads of nature in North America. It has, or at least had, nearly everything. Like an Amazon forest the original vegetation was sometimes dense, sometimes open, and well populated with wild animals. But men came and tore out the heart of it, took away the trees, tilled the soil and tried to extract from the ground every ounce of oil that they could. Only a portion of the true Texas remains, but in a few places such as the Big Thicket and Aransas National Wildlife Refuge we can still see some of the natural crossroads effects. In the Big Thicket alone, 2,000 species of native plants grow: silverbell, beech and magnolia from the east, baldcypress and water tupelo from the south, bur oak and slippery elm from the north, and mesquite, catclaw and soapberry from the west.

One of the most characteristic species is saw-palmetto, a palm with sharp-edged, fan-shaped leaves. Abundant in the Southeast, it usually forms low thickets in pine or oak forests, though it may grow to a height of 25 feet. Under their protecting fronds armadillos scurry about and dig for insects or hunt for carrion. And perhaps a few ocelots remain in some forgotten vale to take cover under palmetto shelter.

A few of the wilder parts of the state are being conserved, as in Big Bend and Guadalupe Mountains National Parks, and Padre Island National Seashore. On lands unprotected, nature makes valiant attempts at beautification. Subtropical oak and cactus forests stretch for miles throughout the southern portion of the state, and bright red fruits of the prickly pear become almost as handsome as its flowers. Massed displays of Texas bluebonnets, a lupine, paint the land a vivid sky blue. And along the southernmost Rio Grande, shared with Mexico, is the entrance to an exotic world of green jays and chachalacas, and such trees as anaqua, ebony, chapatillo and panalero.

Captivated by these enclaves of wild and natural beauty, we are inclined to urge Texans to bring back more of them.

88

Wide Deltas and Winding Bayous

Photographed by Thase Daniel,
Andreas Feininger and Robert Perron

91. Duckweed covers the water and Spanish moss hangs from the trees in a Louisiana bayou near the Mississippi River (Thase Daniel)

92. Water lilies on a Louisiana bayou (Andreas Feininger)

93. A white-tailed buck crosses a Louisiana pond in winter

94. A purple gallinule hunts for insects on Grassy Lake, Arkansas

95. Male and female cattle egrets at nest with young on Avery Island, Louisiana (93-95 by Thase Daniel)

96. Aerial view of bayous in a marsh of the Mississippi delta (Robert Perron)

Down in Louisiana, thousands of people gather from time to time for crayfish-digging jubilees—which says something about the biological productivity of muddy marshes and winding bayous. Looking into the waters, our eyes confirm it: clouds of tiny fish, schools of larger silvery-sided species turning and flashing sunlight through the murk, turtles swimming, crabs surfacing, alligators silently prowling.

Marshes of *Spartina* grass stretch to the level horizon, and where the waters have not been stained from overflowing petroleum wells, flocks of egrets and ibises gather in the orange of dawn to check out new concentrations of fish. Farther inland, especially up the Mississippi River valley, great marshes occupy the lowlands, and in time of flood they may become wide lakes, even though far back from the usual river banks. In Arkansas wildlife refuges live forest animals, such as deer, that occasionally venture out into the marshes. But whether inland or coastal, the marshlands and bayous have fragile systems of life that are vulnerable to even slight alterations.

Construction of ship channels has altered the natural balance between salt water and fresh, with the result that cypresses have died, and where the Sabine River meets the sea they stand as lone white snags in the marshlands. A tough, tooth-bladed sedge known as sawgrass used to be distributed widely until a hurricane brushed the coast with fine salty spray and failed to follow with cleansing rains. The sawgrass, seared, nearly disappeared. And as for bulrushes, they have been diminished by nutrias, large rodents from South America. With all that and marsh fires, the vulnerable ecosystem would seem to be endangered, and perhaps it is. But the marshes and bayous, like all seacoast environments, have a capacity for surviving harsh conditions. At least in the principal wildlife refuges along the Gulf of Mexico coast—Sabine, Aransas, and Laguna Atascosa—nature's resilience may help to restore a little of the natural balance that existed centuries ago.

The Tall-Grass Prairie

Photographed by Patricia Caulfield and Ed Bry

America has many prairies, and even though only patches remain of the original Midwest plains, a few wild open stretches persist. In addition to the well-known rolling grasslands, there are prairies in badlands, sand hills, "staked plains," seacoasts, mesas, and even in wide openings in forests of pine. They are covered by tall grass, short grass, bunch grass, big sand grass, sagebrush, blackbrush, or any of a thousand other species.

Although big sky and emptiness are familiar traits, the prairies possess a seemingly infinite number of pockets, or microhabitats, of different character. As we walk through a cottonwood grove along a snaking creek, the voices of warblers drift through the dell like the resonant notes of flutes. On yellowish cliffs overhead the golden eagles build their nests, and beyond lie gentle slopes or flats where prairie dogs pipe their warnings at the advance of intruders.

The prairie has moments of violence—a night of lightning that never stops flashing until the storm is gone; a flood that crashes through quartzite gorges; a lignite vein ignited and burning; a wind whipping sand with incessant fury.

But all these are a part of the prairie, where delicacy also exists, from the first pasqueflower of spring to the millions of black-eyed susans in summer. The mammals to which American prairies originally belonged are still around. Bison, a bit more adaptable to different environments, can live in woods and on plains and mountains, but pronghorns are uniquely designed for wide-open spaces. Their super-sharp vision, the rump-patch signals, the speed unequaled among American mammals, all make them secure where the horizons are far away.

And wherever the sun from a rain-washed sky shines low across patches of lupine and clover to light up distant hills, or brings into relief the ruts of old wagon trails, the original prairie somehow returns, if only for a few nostalgic moments.

97

100

The North Woods

Photographed by Les Blacklock and Tom Algire

In their coldest season the north woods, which in summer seem too delicate and fragile to withstand much depredation, are locked in a grip of snow and ice. The ponds freeze thickly. Darkness falls for more than half the spin of earth. Herbaceous plants lie dead in all but their seeds or roots, and the trees seem frozen, lifeless, bereft of any possible resurrection. Only the silent tracks of mammals and birds suggest that the land still lives.

One morning some open water appears at the edge of the icy ponds. An orange glow brings warmth in the dawn. A mist sifts through the fir and spruce, dissolving the woods and lakes into ghostly sketches. With lengthening days the bloodroot stirs and blooms. A leaf bud reddens, and then the deciduous leaves burst out. In a very short time the forest burgeons into rich, warm masses of life: ferns diverse and diffused on the forest floor, feathery horsetails in the wetter places, intricate fungus on the trees, scarlet lichens among the moss.

So wild are these woods in places that wolf and moose still roam, as also do bear and caribou. On nearly every lake a loon calls vibrantly, receiving echoed answers from other lakes.

By autumn the mood has quieted again, except for melodies of falling water. Red leaves sprinkle the woods like darts of flame; then the prevalence of green becomes orange, as though a sunset had swept through the forest and tinted it various shades of gold. After that, the leaves collect on the ground and the running water is muffled. With winter the trees seem frozen and lifeless, and the ponds are once more gripped by ice.

103

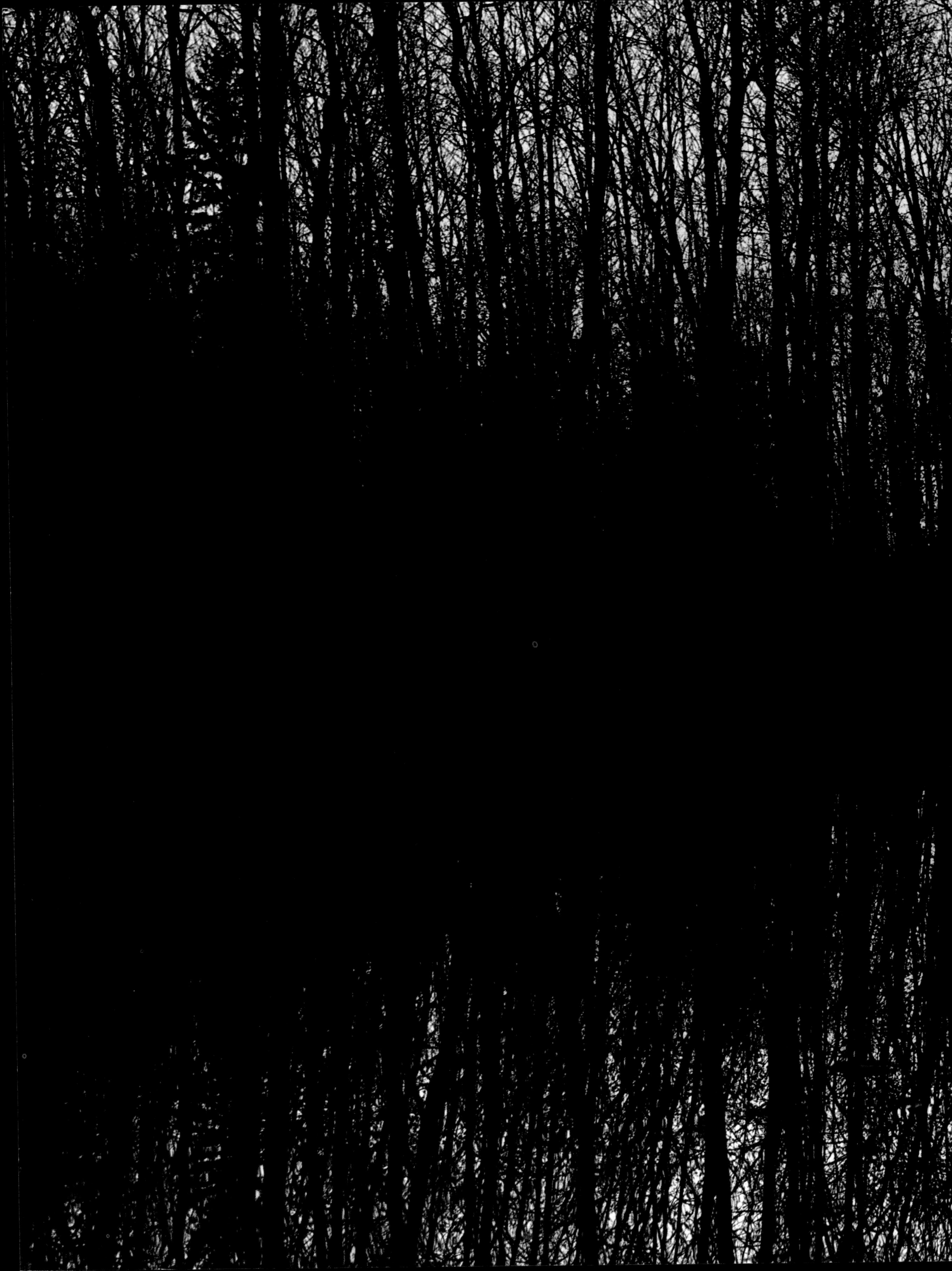

The Heartland

Photographed by Larry West, Les Line and Ron Austing

As sunlight melts the mist, tiny droplets of water cling to webs or roll from maple leaves. The woods and meadows seem released from captivity. Butterflies flutter out of bushes along the river and start their errant flights. A graceful luna moth slowly flies to the trunk of a tree. Chipmunks race along a fallen log and then across a forest floor littered with mushrooms of different sizes, shapes and colors.

Thus begins a day in the central lowlands, where six senses and nine lives would be insufficient to partake fully of the feast nature spreads. Despite the advance of industry and agriculture, uncounted corners of wild land remain along the Ohio, Missouri and Mississippi Rivers. One national wildlife refuge alone measures 284 miles in length. Between the Voyageurs country of Minnesota and the Natchez Trace of Tennessee lie systems of lakes and lowlands, deep deciduous woods, and open meadows that harbor hundreds of thousands of migratory birds each year along the Mississippi Flyway. Artists and philosophers find special messages in the peeling bark of quiet birch groves, or the red autumn landscapes of the Ozarks. They pause to hear the wind in oaks overhanging the winding green rivers, to admire the veins of basswood leaves, to taste the walnut or pecan. Or they go out in the cool of evening when patches of fog steal over the meadows and a giant golden moon begins to climb up out of the woods. In such places, at such times, man, too, is released from captivity.

112

Vermont: Autumn and Winter

Photographed by Sonja Bullaty and Angelo Lomeo

Autumn comes down from the north and settles over the hills of New England like a golden tide. Color surrounds green conifer patches as though they were islets and in turn touches the isolated stands of deciduous trees within the forests and makes them islets of fire amid somber pines. Masses of maple and birch give up their leaves in October and are soon engulfed in layers of snow. Few changes on earth are quite as dramatic; and in few places are the seasons more distinctly identified.

Vermont's Green Mountains, composed of folded schists, gneisses and related rocks into which granites have been intruded, hold lakes that ripple in the summer winds, waters that still fall free and pure, and valleys as green as the vales of Eire. In autumn, however, these uplands might as well be named the Golden Mountains, or the Orange Mountains, or the Scarlet Mountains. When loose leaves flutter through the air they paint the forest floor with yellow. Viburnums, their leaves anointed with royal maroon, produce clusters of scarlet drupes, and closer to the ground grow dwarf dogwoods with equally resplendent bunches of fruit. No matter whether the air is clear or full of mist, whether the sky is blue or gray, whether the breeze is calm or lashing the trees into a fury of rebellion—the color remains, less vivid perhaps, but nonetheless pastel and rich and pervasive.

Whatever the state of the elements, even when there are no leaves on the trees, no color, and no quiet, but only the black of storms or the white of flying snow, the scene is still peaceful, and one is reminded of words attributed to Alfred Nobel: "I want to live among the trees and bushes, silent friends who respect the state of my nerves."

Rocks, Shells and Birds: Maine Island

Photographed by Eliot Porter

Rocks at the edge of the sea never last very long in the passing of geologic eras, but sturdy granites on the coast of Maine resist longer than most before being reduced to sand. The storm-borne waves attack with almost frenetic fury, and it is hard to see how cliffs can withstand such assaults for as many years as they do.

Far more flexible, and nearly as durable, are forms of life that grow at the edge of the sea. As in so many other raw and violent locales, lichens establish themselves as pioneers. They clutch the slick rock surfaces, withstanding wetting and drying, endure the salt, and bear up under the energy of storms. If they can hold on long enough, they may establish a little soil. Other plants become established in this, but they must also be hardy, and perhaps resilient, lest they be ripped from the rocks by thundering waves.

Sea stars, urchins and mollusks have excellent survival capacities in the turbulent water itself, and tidal pools provide a first-hand glimpse of the eternal anomaly: delicacy versus violence. Sea anemones of great beauty establish themselves in caves where water is repeatedly hurled in from the sea and boisterously sloshed around. In gentler pools grow algae, chitons, limpets, periwinkles, barnacles, worms, and crabs, immensely interesting but only introductory to the mass of life that thrives farther out—and down. Now and then on the gravelly shores we find a washed-up lobster, not red as when cooked, but brownish and olive.

We walk on windswept cliffs high above the wild seashore, and find ourselves in deep spruce forests. The path is soft and springy with needles deposited year after year. Beneath a new fir we notice a junco's nest. Inland, we are engulfed by forests of birch and maple, and at times encounter handsome banks of rose pink laurel. Songs of wren and warbler fill the dells.

Even when the coast is submerged in a veil of mist, and the cliffs are lost in curtains of fog, there is still an aura of life and action. Clouds hamper little, for life hangs on and advances and unfolds in spite of the tumultuous waves, the salt sea spray, and the lowering storms.

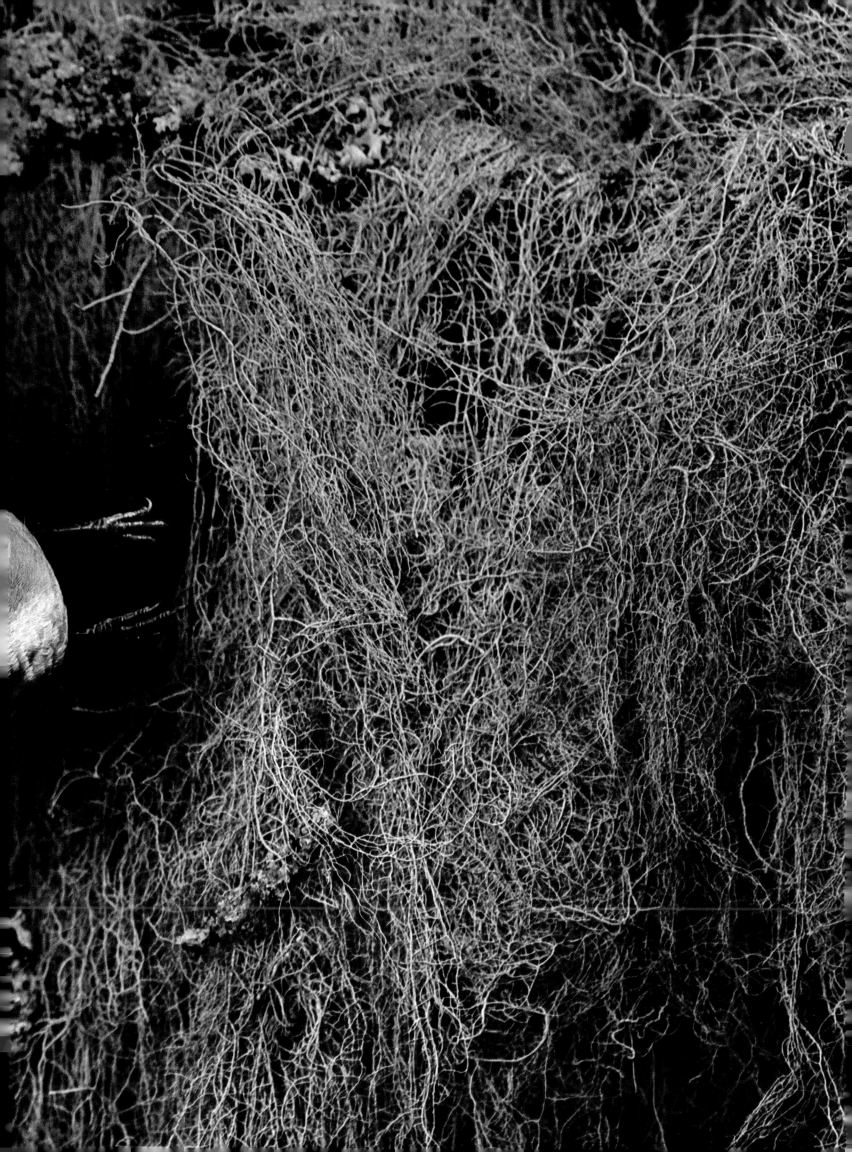

Wide Beaches, High Dunes: Cape Cod

Photographed by Gordon Smith

Were it not for the glaciers that came down across New England, halted, melted, and left their debris behind, we might not have a Cape Cod today. In fact, it is owing as much to glaciers as to the sea that this arm of land thrusting into the Atlantic is so charming and diversified.

Deposits of sand and gravel were built up into high promontories from which we survey the sea and shore, high dunes, pine forests, scrublands, marshlands, moors and sun-flecked waters of sheltered bays. Where giant ice chunks buried under the glacial debris thawed out and melted, the gravels above them sank into depressions now called "kettles." Some hold lakes that look like turquoise gems in a band of green—the forests of pitch pine that surround them. Or the kettles hold marshes where white cedars, among the most unusual conifers on the Atlantic coast, have become close-packed, their arms interlaced.

Everywhere, some kind of action goes on. In May the bushes of beach plum bloom, so white with flowers that they appear to be banks of snow. The herring gull flies up clutching a quahog; it lets the clam fall on rocks so as to shatter the shell and release the delicious contents. Salt marshes, thanks to plentiful plankton, nourish multiple animal forms, from worms to barnacles to great blue herons—a thriving factory producing abundant life.

But always we return to the crashing shore, where even amid the turbulence is life. The receding waves are trailed by a cluster of quick-footed sanderlings, skittering onto the bubbling beach in search of sand fleas. Horseshoe crabs and cases of skate eggs wash up on shore, a hint of the enormous production of pelagic life.

Happily, the beach is still reasonably wild and will remain so. In an era when men were preempting most marshes and building their homes on the beaches, Cape Cod National Seashore was established to protect 27,000 acres of wild land, not only along more than forty miles of beach but in places completely across the Cape. That would have pleased Thoreau, who knew the Cape well. To his mind, the measure of civilization was how well a community conserved its swamps.

122

Under Atlantic Tides

Photographed by Douglas Faulkner

127. Shorthorn sculpin in a cove at Gloucester, Massachusetts

128. Parrot fish and remora, Molasses Reef, Upper Key Largo, Florida

129. Juvenile bluehead wrasses feeding, Molasses Reef, Upper Key Largo

130. Spiny boxfish on White Rock Bank, Upper Key Largo

131. Lobster in a cove near Gloucester, Massachusetts

132. Life on piling near Gloucester

When flounder and cod begin to run, off Massachusetts' eastern coast, the blood of fishermen seems to assume a temperature different from that of ordinary men. By the time the tautog, bass and mackerel course through offshore waters, boat flags fly from Providence to Provincetown, and surfcasters line up along the shores. Occasionally, other marine organisms get mixed up in the angler's catch—dogfish, skates, sand dabs, sculpins, sea robins—and while he regards these as "trash fish," they are only a surface sample of the great subtidal biomass off eastern North America. Best-known crustacean, from North Carolina to Labrador, is the lobster, which lives in rocky caves beneath the surface. Schools of squid prowl about, and in more shallow waters are the crabs—green, blue, pink, orange—as colorful as the sponges, anemones, algae, sea stars, worms and jellyfish in different parts of the same world.

Bright colors are more often associated with subtropical waters around the Florida Keys, and there is no question about the fish there being breathtaking. Life off the keys revolves around rocky outcrops and coral reefs, where holes provide hiding places for fish and other forms of life. The marine fauna, considered tropical despite its location above the Tropic of Cancer, is largely West Indian and South American in character.

Among the larger species are sharks, sailfish, mantas and tuna. But around the reefs live delicate and vividly patterned forms, nourished by plankton and organic material from nearby beds of turtle grass. Some four hundred kinds of fishes have been identified with the coral reef community, starting with flounders in the sand, and clouds of dwarf herring which provide abundant food for larger animals. Swimmers who enter this domain become fascinated by the highly colored angelfish, triggerfish, butterfly fish, parrotfish and sergeant-major. And sometimes they find themselves surrounded by masses of tiny silvery fish, attesting in their numbers to the richness of the ecosystem beneath Atlantic tides.

127

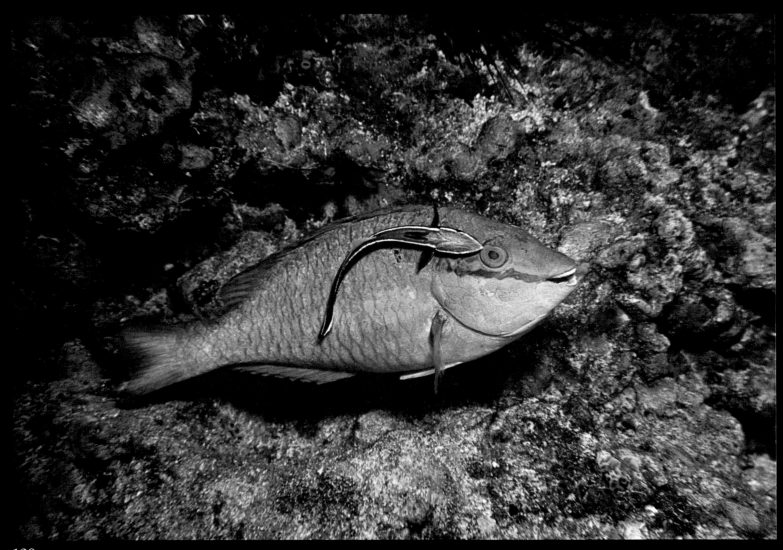

129

130

131

Trees and Winter Brush: The Hudson Highlands

Photographed by Ralph Weiss

It is sometimes difficult to imagine that several of the larger wilderness areas of America are located in the most populous states. New York, for example, has its Adirondack and Catskill Mountains. Even though some of these uplands were once burned over or cut, and the threats of encroachment have still not entirely abated, millions of acres of wild land in them have been preserved. Attempts to stave off waste and ruin began more than a century ago, and the landmark phrase "forever wild" became not only a matter of public philosophy but a part of the state Constitution.

All this resulted in part at least from the diminishing in other places of undisturbed mountain lakes and trails, pure air, quiet, solitude, music of free-tumbling streams, uncluttered forests, and related primeval aspects of the landscape. In the years that have passed since the first legislation in 1885, New York's mountain parks have been provided with trails and canoe routes that lead, figuratively if not literally, into other worlds and other eras.

Hiking up Mount Marcy, for example, we are enclosed in cathedral groves of birch and maple and hemlock. The ground is seldom seen, for layers of duff have covered it, and only dark outcrops of rock break through the accumulation. In the Catskills, forest trails take hikers into light-filled groves of trees, past streams and ravines to waterfalls. Going up, the hiker breaks out of enclosing woods for a walk on a summit ridge or an assault on a mountain peak. But even on reaching the top his taste of success is temporary; in the distance rise other ridges and peaks that he has not yet climbed. And below lie lonely ponds awaiting inspection. He will not be content until, the sooner the better, he beaches his canoe on one of those shores and sets up camp in the hemlock woods. But when he does that he will want to go on again, and there are likely to be more Catskills and wild Adirondacks than he will ever have time to explore. In this case, therefore, the highlands of New York are an infinite wilderness for a restless man.

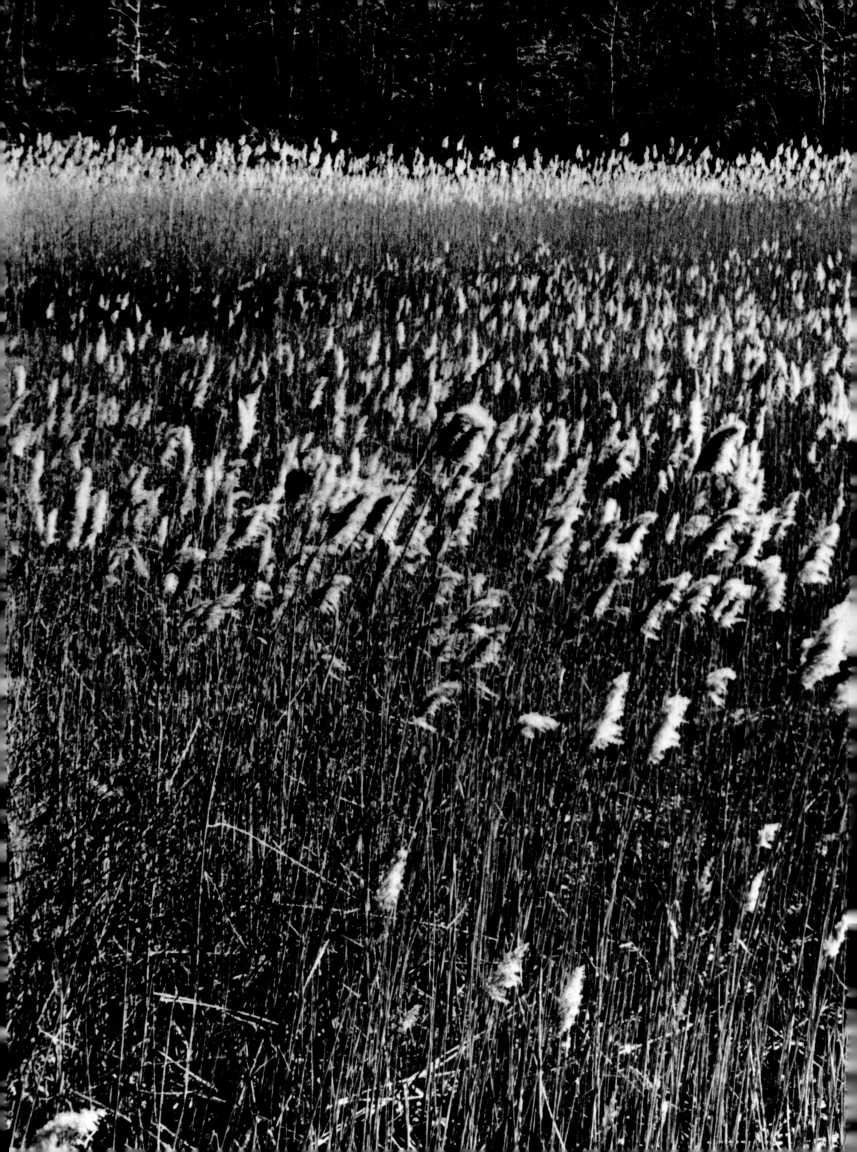

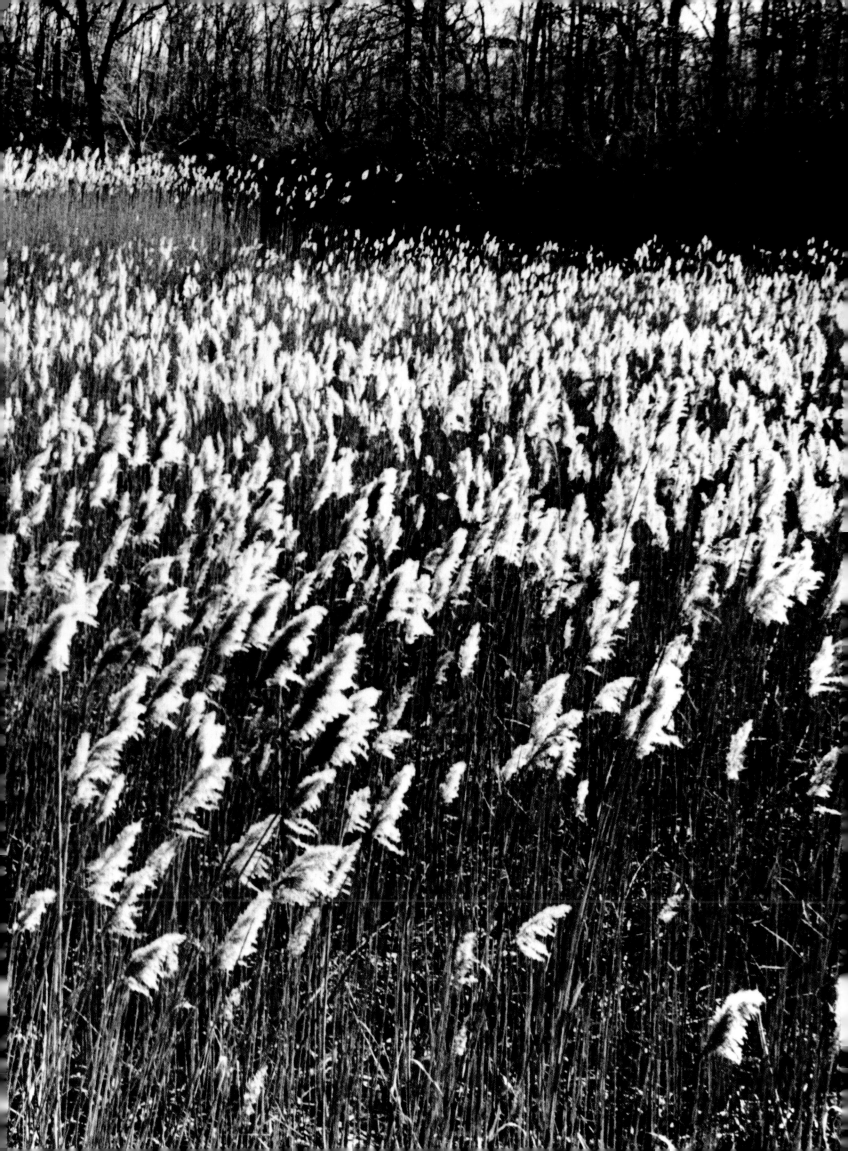

In The Great Smokies

Photographed by William A. Bake, Jr. and Larry West

138. *Big Santeetlah Creek*

139. *Roaring Fork Creek, Great Smoky Mountains National Park (138-139 by William A. Bake, Jr.)*

140. *Southern lady fern (Larry West)*

141. *High shoals in the Appalachee River (William A. Bake, Jr.)*

"This is a good strong land," said the mountain people, "or it wouldn't hold up all the rocks there is around here." The Great Smokies have been in a state of repose for sixty million years and were one of the few North American ranges to escape the ravages of glaciation. As such, their gentle coves and valleys have nurtured plants that came from as far off as China, presumably across now-vanished bridges of land. The summits have harbored spruce and fir characteristic of Canada. And it is a question whether Europe or the Appalachian region has more species of trees. In the Great Smokies alone there are more than 130, of which at least twenty reach greater size than they do anywhere else.

But there can be no question about the consummate loveliness of these mountains at all times of year. The delicate spectacle in spring, when the peaks are painted with countless clusters of purple rhododendron, is matched only by the flowering of Southwest deserts or of upland meadows in the Cascades. Some of the most memorable experiences in the southern Appalachians are to be had along mountain streams, which contain what must be surely the purest, clearest waters anywhere. In hidden shadows, white rhododendrons open their floral bouquets, and the secretive painted trillium unfolds beneath the shrubs. Bell-like flowers of leucothoe are strung out over the bank, and where logs have decayed for centuries is a rich forest floor literally covered with the bright green leaves and coral pink flowers of oxalis. On open spots, in the warmth of the sun, grow masses of bluets, but nature's most sophisticated achievement on these ridges is flame azaleas. Though actually rhododendrons, they have characteristics decidedly different from those of Catawba, sweetbay and dwarf varieties. Their flame-orange petals grace the views of deep blue mountains and valleys, and occasionally their flowers appear in variants of yellow, salmon, maroon and a dozen other shades. The mountains burst with great biological productivity, as stands of immense tulip trees attest, and in autumn the mass of deciduous leaves turns into a jumble of colors—each species with a hue of its own. One visit to such an empire of color and creation confirms our attitude toward the approach of modern civilization: thus far and no farther.

140

Carolina Lowlands

Photographed by Jack Dermid

A few wild swamplands and river bottoms have survived rather well the pressure of agriculture and construction along the Atlantic coastal plain. In the Carolina low country lie estuaries, marshes, sand banks and offshore islands warmed by a subtropic sun and abundant with life. Gnarled oaks adorned with swaying shreds of Spanish moss rise massively above marsh-edge environments, as do great flowering magnolias, and baldcypresses whose thickened trunks dominate hidden swamps. Beyond the bayberry and holly, such birds as laughing gulls drift along on breezes above the shifting shores and waving sea oats. Inland one hears penetrating calls of quail, and now and then may glimpse a flock of wild turkeys ambling among the grasses. In numerous localities the mockingbird assumes command—depending on how many jays are present. By the millions birds take refuge from winter, though frosts do reach these regions.

Well fitted into the rich ecosystems are uncounted numbers of insects, not the least of which are mosquitoes. As for reptiles, we find alligators, turtles and more than forty species of snakes. There is infinitely more than human eyes can absorb, and one feels almost compelled to build a small discreet houseboat that could drift along the waterways and permit uninterrupted observations of the wild lives that few men know about. Nature, as always, is unhurried. The opossum has no schedule. The terrapin is timeless. The eagle flies without a deadline. Only when hurricanes roll across the marshes and forests do Carolina lowlands change very rapidly. And even then, the natural grandeur

143

144

145

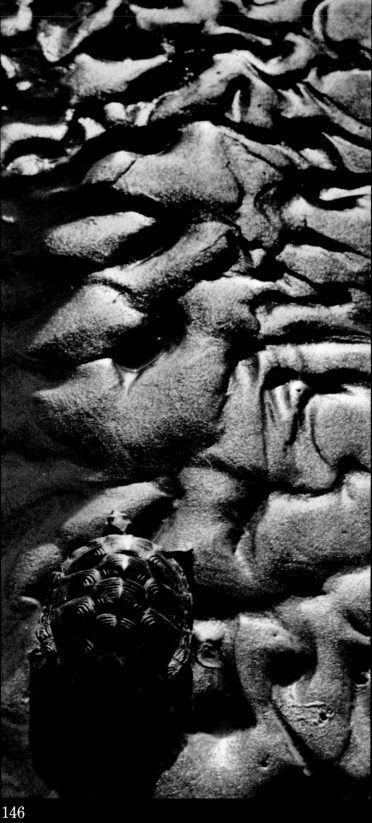

146

147

148

Where the trade winds blow and the climate is kind to delicate forms of life, nature has created highly sophisticated but precariously balanced ecosystems of mangrove swamps, sea islands, salt flats, and freshwater meadows. Not many species of mammals live in these environments, save for deer, raccoons, the rare manatee, and a few others. Reptiles are prominent, primarily the alligator, and there are occasional American crocodiles. But for the most part, southern Florida's shores are domains of fish, birds and insects.

In shallow emerald bays, warmed by the sun and nourished by currents from seaward and landward, the richness and abundance of nutrients is sufficient to produce great numbers of fish, insects, and crustaceans. Were it not for these aquatic nurseries—bights, bays, bayous, mangrove waterways, and inland marshes—most birds would not be there. As Floridians long ago learned, wild birds are not saved without the land on which they live and the waters in which they feed.

By far the most beautifully plumaged birds, flamingoes and roseate spoonbills, live in shallow waters where with their specially adapted beaks they sift through muds for tiny shellfish and other small marine life. Pelicans dive in deep water or shallow in order to scoop up fish. Reddish egrets, clowns of the bays, prance around in shallow waters, darting in all directions at once, so it seems, to pursue the fishes, frogs and shrimp that keep them alive. Some herons and egrets, along with wood ibises that occasionally circle in great flocks high in the sky, fly inland to marshes where they spend the day hunting for fish and aquatic reptiles.

If this seems an earthly paradise, it isn't, quite, and one drawback is the hurricane. Big fragile birds are at a decided disadvantage when the wind reaches fifty miles an hour, much less a hundred and fifty, and so hundreds of them are slammed into the mangroves and killed. Frost is another problem. Storms at the wrong time can disturb the nesting process. Drought shrivels ponds where birds get food. And there is the matter of contaminants in the sea.

But withal, it is a relatively safe and carefree life for big water birds—as long as they have a few million acres of undisturbed land and sea.

149

151

Georgia Sea Islands

Photographed by James P. Valentine

154. Swamp on Ossabaw Island, Georgia

155. Aquatic plants in a fresh-water swamp on Big Cumberland Island, Georgia

156. Desert on Big Cumberland Island

157. Desert on Big Cumberland Island

They are born of the sea—and in time destroyed by it. Or caressed by tropical breezes—and then destroyed by them. Along this Atlantic shore, so vulnerable to tropical storms, the offshore islands are hardly for man or beast when at their harshest. Yet life abounds in a gradually thickening succession from sea to sound.

At the outermost edge, where the gales come whistling in untamed, grow pioneer plants that have to withstand not only high-velocity winds but a great deal of salt in the air. If rains do not wash off the salt soon after it is sprayed on the vegetation, the leaves or needles of coastal plants may "burn" to an ominous brown and eventually wither.

Fortunately, fresh rains are frequent, but they sink into the dunes and vanish, and are thus of only marginal value to plants. The result is a desert where cactus and yucca survive. Shrubs anchor in dunes, but the sands soon blow out from under them. Or the dunes march inland, engulf the trees, and move on, leaving bent and broken snags.

Finally stabilized by sea oats and spurges, the dunes shield inner vales from flying salt, and in the protected places small oaks and palmettos manage to thrive. Farther inland, the trees are taller and the woods more dense. Oaks, even though twisted, grow larger, and become the host to an army of ferns or vines of wild grape.

Then, deep in the interior of the islands, high palms festooned with "Spanish moss" become a dominant part of the forest. Alligators search for raccoons, and woodpeckers rattle the silence.

Finally, in the marshes and ponds on the inland side of the island, new soil is formed by the growth and decay of plants. But even these sheltered woods and lagoons are vulnerable to the most destructive storms. How long each sea island lasts depends on the whim of the wind and the fury

The Great Swamp: Okefenokee

Photographed by Yvona and Momo Momatiuk and Leonard Lee Rue III

This watery wilderness in southern Georgia is hardly as dark or brooding today as it seemed to early explorers, who called it Ouaquaphenogaw and largely shunned it. Light from sunbeams passes through Spanish moss on baldcypress trees and illumines the shrubs with a kind of green incandescence. White water-lilies, yellow spatterdock, purple swamp iris—many species of flowers enrich the greenery.

The tinted brown waters flow with a respectable current, for Okefenokee is a mass of fresh water thirty-two miles in diameter, part of which goes southeastward to become the historic St. Mary's River, and part southwestward to become the legendary Suwannee. Okefenokee is also a vast peat bog. Some of its seventy islands are floating masses of peat whose trees bob up and down as we walk on them.

Because only a few canoe routes lead through this vast wilderness area, nobody knows how many thousands of alligators it shelters, or bears or raccoons or crayfish. Grand Prairie, a water wilderness speckled with lily pads, is home for rare Florida sandhill cranes. The entire swamp is a bird paradise.

Rather than a forbidding place, Okefenokee is now a wildlife refuge so popular that entry has had to be restricted lest too many visitors damage the natural values. It merits the kind of praise that William Bartram, a naturalist, bestowed on such places in the 1770s: "What a beautiful display of vegetation is here before me!"

The Everglades

Photographed by James H. Carmichael, Jr., Patricia Caulfield, Ed Cooper, Ray O. Green, Caulion Singletary, and Kojo Tanaka

161. American egret in sawgrass marsh, Everglades National Park (James H. Carmichael, Jr.)

162. Anhinga seizing a fish (Caulion Singletary)

163. Osprey in the Everglades (Kojo Tanaka)

164. Anhinga (Ray O. Green)

165. Florida cypress trees in Big Cypress Swamp (Ed Cooper)

166. Egrets and spoonbills (Patricia Caulfield)

The "glades" in "Everglades" are sawgrass marshes through which, in seasons of rain, vast flows of fresh water circulate on their way to the sea. This widest kind of river moves slowly on Florida's coastal plain; six inches is a high elevation six miles from the sea. While still far inland the river encounters salt water, mixes with it, and eventually passes through mangrove mazes into Florida Bay.

The glades are difficult for men to cross because of the treacherous, sharp, rock and the razor edges of sawgrass. Only where rocky islands protrude above the water do forests grow.

To open the glades and keep them open is no easy task, but nature has several approaches, principally water and fire. Were it not for rapidly advancing sheets of flame, when the sawgrass catches fire, hardwood forests might spread unchecked and put an end to the glades.

The 1.4 million acres encompassed by Everglades National Park contain distinctive habitats: forests of pine and palmetto, freshwater sloughs, mounds called hammocks with tropical trees like gumbo-limbo and paurotis palm, labyrinths of mangrove, coastal prairies with cactus and yucca, and shallow bays off shore.

Some habitats are affected by fire, some by cold, some by salinity of water. All are at the mercy of hurricanes, especially the coastal prairie, where buttonwood trees receive the unchecked fury of winds and waters. Few saline succulent ground plants have replaced the white snags that remain from the storm of 1935.

Boardwalks enable human beings to enter a few of these wild habitats discreetly. If we keep to the trail, all go about their business: egrets spearing fish, alligators sunning on river banks, cottonmouths coiled in clumps of grass, gallinules walking on lily pads.

Or in a canoe on remote water trails we are witness to tarpon leaping out of lakes, or rare crocodiles submerging in the milky waters of the bay.

The Everglades long remained undisturbed because they were considered useless and inaccessible. When men began eyeing their potentials for hunting, farming and settling, the public rose up in efforts to keep them wild. Subsequent threats provoked a national uprising in their defense. The Everglades, in their serenity an unlikely battleground, have tested the resolve of citizens nationwide. The results have confirmed the public ideal that in its wilder places is the real America.

161

162

163

Notes on the Photographers

The numbers in parentheses refer to photographs

Tom Algire (104) grew up in the Bethesda, Maryland area but now lives near Gleason, Wisconsin, hard by a trout stream and woods still rich in beaver, otter, and deer. He has been a photographer since graduation from college. His nature photography has appeared in *Wisconsin Trails, Outdoor World,* and other magazines.

Ron Austing (110) is known for his action photographs of birds of prey. A county park ranger in Ohio, he is the author of *The Red-tailed Hawk* and *I Went to the Woods* and co-author of *The World of the Great Horned Owl.*

William A. Bake, Jr. (138-139, 141), a native of Michigan, teaches environmental education at the University of Georgia.
He photographs with the hope that glimpsing "remnants of what once was, we can know what might be left for tomorrow."
His photographs and articles have appeared in nature and photography magazines.

Les Blacklock's (103, 105-106) boyhood in the village of Moose Lake, Michigan, led—after study of photography at the University of Minnesota—to his career as a wildlife photographer. Along with photographs in national magazines he has produced a motion picture *Deer Live with Danger* and collaborated with the famous northwoods author Sigurd F. Olson on a book, *The Hidden Forest.*

Jim Bones (85-90) describes himself as a "writer/ photographer/teacher" devoted to showing "the beauty of wholeness expressed in the earth's remaining wild places." He was born in Louisiana, studied at the University of Texas, and is Artist in Residence at the J. Frank Dobie Ranch at the University. He is author of *Texas Earth Surfaces.*

Dennis Brokaw (34-37) majored in mathematics at the University of San Diego and became a flight test engineer, but later turned to photography, mainly of nature.
His work has appeared in many publications and a book of his will appear shortly.

Richard Weymouth Brooks (59-60), a Californian, became a photographer during the Korean War. He does general photography but finds desert photography serves both his economic and personal needs. His work appears increasingly in nature publications.

Dean Brown (4, 10, 14, 20), a Virginian, studied music but in 1967 turned to photographing landscapes and people professionally. His landscape work has appeared in many national publications.

Fred Bruemmer (18-19) came to Canada from Latvia in 1951 and worked on newspapers as a photographer and reporter. In 1962 he became a free-lancer specializing in the Arctic. He has written 300 articles and three books, including *Encounters with Arctic Animals*.

Ed Bry (99) has worked for the Game and Fish Department in his native North Dakota for 23 years, first as a game warden and then as editor-photographer of the North Dakota *Outdoors*. His pictures have appeared in *Audubon*, *Field and Stream*, and other publications.

Sonja Bullaty and Angelo Lomeo (114-116) are a husband-and-wife team. She was born in Prague, Czechoslovakia, and he in New York. Essentially self-taught as photographers, their picture essays, chiefly of nature, have appeared in *Audubon*, *Life*, *Horizon*, and in various wildlife books.

James H. Carmichael, Jr. (161) was born in Georgia. After five years as instructor in anthropology at the University of North Carolina, he became a photographer, concentrating on close-up views of nature. His work has appeared in many nature magazines.

Patricia Caulfield (2, 97-98, 100-102, 166) was raised in Iowa and graduated from the University of Rochester. She joined the staff of *Modern Photography* and became executive editor but resigned in 1967 to devote herself to nature photography and conservation. She is the creator of an outstanding Sierra Club book on the Everglades. She has spent much time photographing what remains of the tall-grass prairie.

David Cavagnaro's (43-48, 70-74) study of entomology in California colleges led, in 1961, to his joining an entomological expedition to Southeast Asia and Australia and, later, similar expeditions. Since winning a *Life* photo contest in 1970 he has carried out photographic assignments for Time-Life books. He has published two books, *Living Water* and *This Living Earth*. He is resident biologist at the Audubon Canyon Ranch.

Ron Church (38-42), a Californian, was chief pilot-photographer for the Westinghouse deep-sea program. He was also the only American member of Jacques Yves Cousteau's team on the oceanographic ship *Calypso*, filming TV and book material under Alaska ice, in the Mediterranean and elsewhere. His work has appeared in many publications.

Ed Cooper (6-8, 57-58, 165) was brought up in New York City but, after an early trip west, wrote: "Seeing the Grand Tetons was a spiritual discovery, like being reborn." After graduating from the University of Washington, he worked on Wall Street but then moved to Seattle and became a photographer. He was the major contributor to the Seattle Mountaineers' *The Alpine Lakes* and has appeared in other wilderness publications.

Steve Crouch (75). After schooling from Texas to Oklahoma and graduate study at the University of Chicago, he turned to photography in 1948. His pictures, chiefly of the Pacific Coast, have appeared in many exhibitions and periodicals, and a book of his photographs and text, *Steinbeck Country*, will be published shortly.

William G. Damroth (149-153), a New Yorker, was educated at Stevens Institute of Technology. After a career as head of an investment firm he retired from business and became a wildlife photographer. He has published a book, *Passport to Nature*, and his work has appeared in various magazines. He lives on Florida's Gulf Coast.

Thase Daniel (83, 91, 93-95), born in Arkansas, studied music and later taught piano in Louisiana. Passionately devoted to photographing nature, especially the birds and flowers of the bayous, she has contributed to leading nature publications.

Jack Dermid (142-148) studied wildlife management at North Carolina State and Oregon State universities. As an editor of *Wildlife in North Carolina* and now as assistant professor of biology at the University of North Carolina he is devoted to wildlife protection. His work has appeared in many magazines and he is co-author of the forthcoming *The World of the Wood Duck.*

Douglas Faulkner (127-132), internationally known underwater photographer, studied marine biology at the University of Miami and then began his career with a trip to the South Pacific in 1962. His photographs have been on permanent display at the American Museum of Natural History, the Smithsonian Institution and elsewhere and have been featured in publications here and abroad. He is co-author of *The Hidden Sea.*

Andreas Feininger (92), internationally famous photographer, was trained as an architect in Germany but became a photographer when he moved to Stockholm in 1933. Coming to New York in 1940 he was a *Life* photographer until 1962 when he began to devote himself to his own projects. He has published 22 books, chiefly on nature but also on photographic subjects. His work is in many museums.

Jerry Gentry (79, 81), educated in Texas, and now living in Pasadena, California, has been photographing the Southwest deserts since 1966. Over 200 of his photos have appeared in such publications as *National Wildlife* and *Encyclopaedia Britannica.*

Ray O. Green (164) grew up in Miami, Florida. He manages a camera shop and nature photography has become his prime avocation. His photographs

of the Everglades have appeared in several national magazines.

Philip Hyde (9), a native of San Francisco, studied photography under Ansel Adams, Minor White and Edward Weston. Since 1962 he has illustrated seven books, including *Slickrock* and *An Island Called California,* and he has appeared in many other publications.
He now concentrates on the "increasingly pressured" Western wildlands.

Les Line (108), born in a small town in Michigan, won many prizes for news photography and conservation reporting before becoming editor of *Audubon* magazine in 1966. The magazine has since become known for its excellent graphics, color photography and environmental reporting. Line's own wildlife photography has appeared in many magazines.

Yvona and Momo Momatiuk (159-160), a husband-and-wife team from Poland, photographed together until his death in an avalanche late in 1972. He had been a mountain climber and the author of guide books, mainly on ecology. She has been an editor of architectural publications and was her husband's climbing partner. Their photographs appeared in many magazines.

David Muench (27-28, 61-69, 76-78), a Californian, attended several universities before studying photography at the Art Center in Los Angeles. From the first he has had a total involvement in photographing the Western landscape. He has published *California* (with Ray Atkeson), 1970; *Arizona,* 1971; *Timberline Ancients,* 1972; and he is preparing books on Utah and Colorado. He has appeared in many other publications.

Charlie Ott (12, 17) became interested in wildlife as a Wisconsin farm boy. After a stay in Denver, he left for Alaska, and has been on the staff of Mt. McKinley National Park ever since. His pictures have appeared in *Wild Alaska* and other conservation publications.

Robert Perron (1, 96) studied art at the Yale School of Art and Architecture and now combines aerial and architectural photography. Since 1963 he has made a specialty of water landscapes and now has a collection ranging from Cape Cod to San Francisco. His photographs have appeared in both nature and architectural publications.

Willis Peterson (80) has been dedicated to nature since growing up in Colorado Springs. He did graduate work in audiovisual education at Arizona State University, became a nature photographer and writer, and directs the photographic department at Glendale (Ariz.) Community College. His work has appeared in many publications.

Eliot Porter (117-121) graduated from Harvard Medical School and taught biochemistry at Harvard, but in 1939 he gave up science for photography.
He soon had a major exhibition at Alfred Stieglitz's celebrated An American Place and has since established himself as one of the great nature photographers. He has won many awards, and his work has been exhibited in major museums from New York to San Francisco. He is the author of ten books (five of them for the Sierra Club), including *Forever Wild, The Adirondacks, Down the Colorado,* and (as co-author) *The African Experience.* He lives in Santa Fe.

Betty Randall (21-22) grew up in Berkeley, California and took an M.A. in biochemistry at the university there. After more than twenty years of laboratory research work, she began a career as a photographer. Her work has appeared in leading nature publications, including Chanticleer Press books and *Audubon* magazine.

Bill Ratcliffe (84) was born and still lives in Utah. After attending classes in motion picture photography and script writing, he became a photographer. His work, focussing on "the beauty of small, insignificant things that others overlook," has appeared in many publications, and he has published a volume of his wildflower photos.

Leonard Lee Rue III (158) lives and works in the Delaware Water Gap area and has devoted his life to wildlife writing, lecturing and photography. His articles and photos have appeared in 400 publications and he has published over a dozen books on the animals of North America.

Caulion Singletary (162) has a printing business in Homestead, Florida, but the photographing of nature, and especially birds, has long been his main avocation. His work has appeared in major nature publications.

Gordon S. Smith (122-126) was born and educated in England, but now lives on Cape Cod and is devoted to portraying the Cape's interrelationship with man. Author as well as photographer, his work appears regularly in many publications, including *Infinity* and *Camera 35.*

Charles Steinhacker (53-56), a New Yorker, was educated at Dartmouth and New York University. His hope in his nature photography is that he is helping to preserve whatever is still unspoiled. He has published *Superior: Portrait of a Living Lake* and was the main photographer in *Yellowstone: A Century of the Wilderness Idea.* Two other books by him will be published shortly.

Kojo Tanaka (3, 15-16, 49-52, 163) is Japan's leading animal photographer. Out of his photographic journeys have come his books on the wildlife of the United States (including Alaska), Canada, Japan, Africa and Latin America. Educated as a zoologist, he combines a knowledge of animal behavior with an insistence on photographing animals in their native environment.

James P. Valentine (154-157) thinks of himself as using the poetry of the camera to create a conservation-oriented view of our environment, as, for example, in his exhibit, "Guale, The Golden Coast of Georgia." He is a native of Highlands, North Carolina, where he has established a conservation center, the Quest Foundation.

Ralph Weiss (133-137), a New Yorker, has hiked in the Hudson Highlands since childhood. Although trained as a geologist at the Missouri School of Mines, he has been a photographer since 1961. He teaches in his own workshop and at the New York Phoenix School of Design. His photographs have appeared in many publications and are in various museum collections.

Larry West (107, 109, 111-113, 140) lives beside a woodlot a mile from where he was born in Mason, Michigan. His aim as a nature photographer has been "to find the leaf that stands for all leaves and the perfect moment to photograph it." He has appeared in many books and magazines and has lectured on photography.

Steven C. Wilson (22-26, 31, 33, 82) is an Iowan who majored in fisheries at the University of Washington and now lives in Washington. A student of animal behavior, he attempts through films (he has made five) and widely published photographs to "increase man's awareness of the other living things on our planet."

Don Worth (29-30, 32) began his career as a concert pianist and composer but shifted to photography and worked under Ansel Adams in California. He is associate professor of art, teaching photography, at California State University, San Francisco. His black-white prints are in major museum collections, and have appeared in many publications.

Michael Wotton (11, 13) was born in England and studied forestry at the University of Wales. After coming to the University of Washington he settled in Washington State and is now director of the Weyerhaeuser Company Forestry Research Center. His photographs, especially of birds, have appeared in many publications, including those of Chanticleer Press and the Audubon Society.

Bradford Washburn (5), distinguished geographer and explorer, has been Director of the Museum of Science (Boston) since 1939. His photographs and articles on the mountains of Alaska have been featured in *National Geographic* and many other publications. They have brought him wide recognition, including honorary degrees from six universities.